Jackie Robinson
— Amazing Athlete and Activist —

written by Darlene R. Stille   illustrated by Richard Stergulz

Beginner
Biographies

Content Consultant:
Hoyt Purvis, Professor of Journalism,
University of Arkansas

visit us at www.abdopublishing.com

Published by Magic Wagon, a division of the ABDO Group, PO Box 398166, Minneapolis, MN 55439.

Printed in the United States of America, North Mankato, Minnesota.
092012
012013

♲ THIS BOOK CONTAINS AT LEAST 10% RECYCLED MATERIALS.

Text by Darlene R. Stille
Illustrations by Richard Stergulz
Edited by Holly Saari
Series design and cover production by Emily Love
Interior production by Craig Hinton

Library of Congress Cataloging-in-Publication Data

Stille, Darlene R.
  Jackie Robinson : amazing athlete and activist / written by Darlene R. Stille ; illustrated by Richard Stergulz.
       p. cm. – (Beginner biographies)
  Includes index.
  ISBN 978-1-61641-940-0
1. Robinson, Jackie, 1919-1972–Juvenile literature. 2. African American baseball players–Biography–Juvenile literature. 3. Baseball players–United States–Biography–Juvenile literature. 4. Political activists–United States–Biography–Juvenile literature. I. Stergulz, Richard ill. II. Title.
  GV865.R6S84 2013
  796.357092–dc23
  [B]   2012023802

Table of Contents

Jackie was the youngest
of five children.

A Tough Beginning

Jackie Robinson's family lived in a small town in Georgia. They were very poor. They rented a piece of land to farm. Jackie was born on January 31, 1919. One day when Jackie was little, his father left. Soon after, the family moved to Pasadena, California.

Learning to Be Proud

Jackie grew up during a time when many white people looked down on African Americans. Some whites thought people like Jackie were not as good because they had dark skin. This type of thinking is called racism.

Some white people called Jackie names. Jackie's mom told him those names weren't true. She taught him that racism was wrong. She taught all of her children to be proud of who they were.

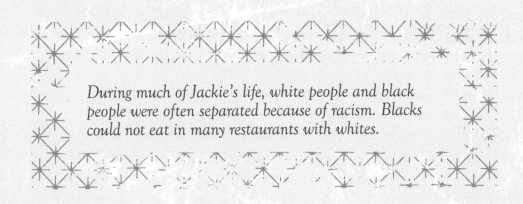

During much of Jackie's life, white people and black people were often separated because of racism. Blacks could not eat in many restaurants with whites.

Blacks often had to use different drinking fountains and restrooms from whites.

Jackie became a leader of his neighborhood friends.

As Jackie grew up, he played a lot of sports. He was always good at what he played. Jackie lived on Pepper Street. He and his friends called themselves the Pepper Street Gang. Sometimes they played pranks and got into trouble with the police.

Jackie had several adults in his life who looked out for him, including Reverend Karl Downs. Karl was the pastor at the Robinsons' church. He helped Jackie stay away from the gang. Jackie chose to focus on sports instead. He joined the football team in high school. His talent shined. He was made team quarterback in 1935 and 1936.

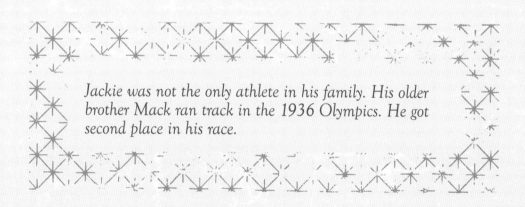

Jackie was not the only athlete in his family. His older brother Mack ran track in the 1936 Olympics. He got second place in his race.

Jackie went to Pasadena Junior College after high school. He became a star in four sports: football, track, basketball, and baseball. Many bigger colleges wanted him to play for their teams.

Jackie then went to the University of California at Los Angeles (UCLA) on a scholarship. He ran track and played varsity football, baseball, and tennis. Varsity teams are for the best players. He was the first student ever to play on four varsity teams in one year.

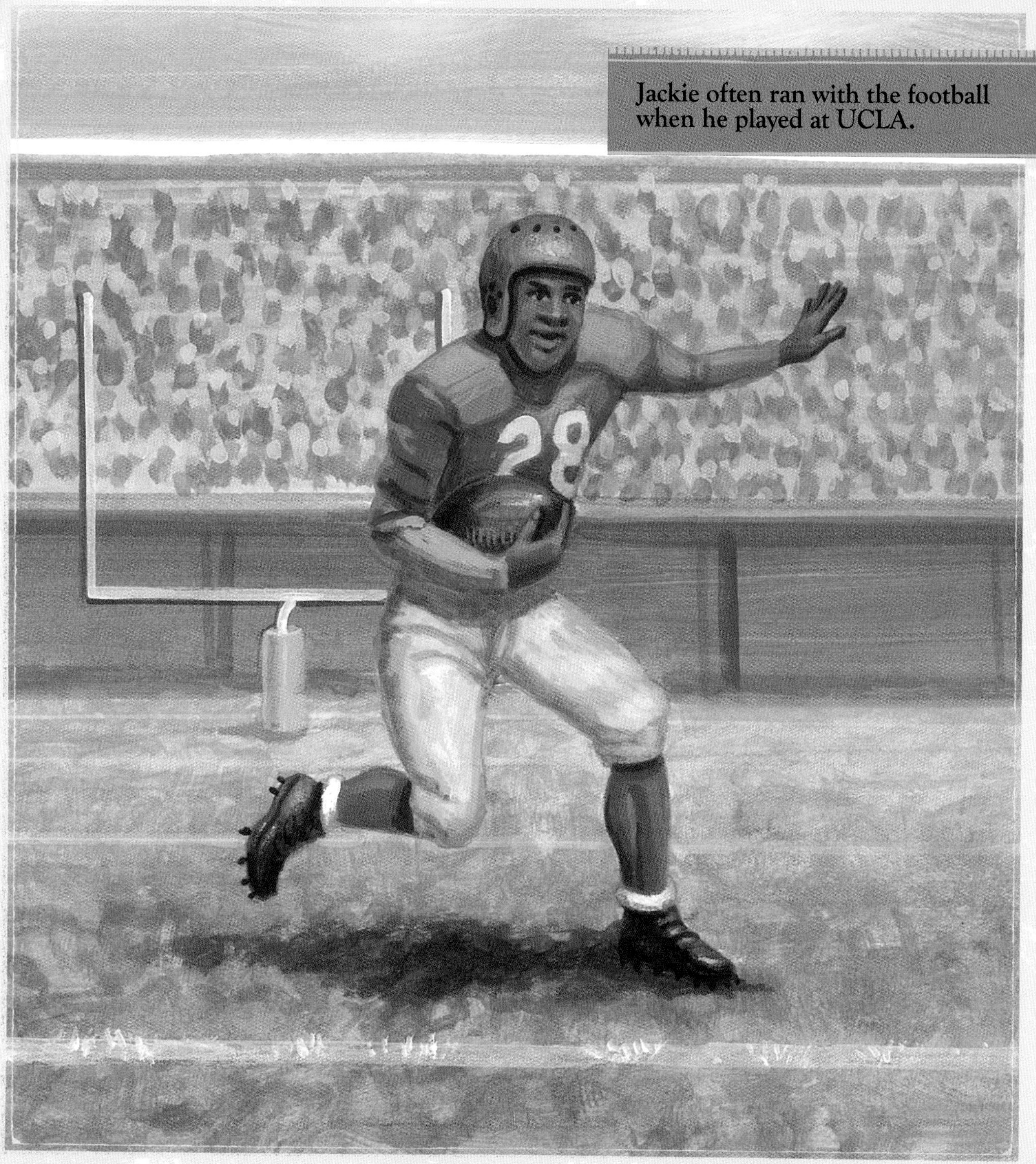

Jackie often ran with the football when he played at UCLA.

Army Life

In 1941, the United States entered World War II. Robinson joined the army to help out. He became a second lieutenant. At the time, only a few other African Americans had reached that rank.

African Americans suffered discrimination in the army. Sometimes they were in separate units from whites. Robinson could not play on the army's sports teams because he was African-American.

One day, he was told to go to the back of a bus. This is where African Americans usually had to sit. He refused. Robinson was arrested and charged with not following orders. He was found not guilty. After this, Robinson was able to leave the army.

Robinson got into trouble when he refused to move to the back of the bus.

Negro Leagues

In the early 1900s, major and minor league baseball teams would not let African Americans play. So, African Americans started their own teams and formed the Negro Leagues.

After Robinson left the army, he began playing baseball in the Negro Leagues for the Kansas City Monarchs. Robinson did not like playing in the league. He didn't like anything that did not let blacks and whites be treated as equals. The Negro Leagues were unfair. Players were not paid as much as players in all-white leagues. Robinson was almost ready to quit.

Robinson played second base for the Kansas City Monarchs.

Rickey was glad to have
Robinson join the Dodgers.

Then Branch Rickey learned about Robinson. Rickey was the head of the Brooklyn Dodgers, a Major League Baseball team from New York. Rickey thought Robinson was very talented. He asked Robinson to play for the Dodgers.

Robinson would be the first African-American player in modern Major League Baseball. Rickey warned Robinson that white fans and players would insult him. Robinson said that he could take it. In October 1945, he signed on with the Brooklyn Dodgers.

Rachel visited with Jackie
before and after games.

Minor Leagues

Baseball players often play in the minors before they move up to the majors. In 1946, Robinson played on a minor league team owned by the Dodgers. He moved to Canada to play with the Montreal Royals. That same year, Robinson married his college sweetheart, Rachel Isum. The couple liked Canada. Discrimination was not as harsh there.

Robinson was a great hitter and a very good fielder. He helped his team win its league championship. Other people noticed, and Robinson was called up to the major leagues.

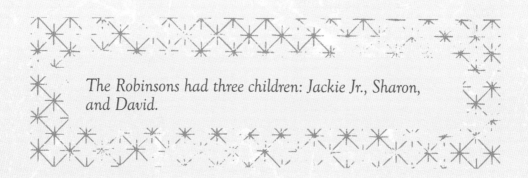

The Robinsons had three children: Jackie Jr., Sharon, and David.

Robinson was great at stealing bases.

20

Major Leagues

On April 15, 1947, Robinson played his first game for the Brooklyn Dodgers. It was an important event. He was the only African-American player in Major League Baseball.

At first, some Dodgers players and fans did not like him playing on the team. But they soon saw that Robinson was a star. He could hit home runs. He could run quickly. He stole more bases than any other player in his team's league.

Robinson hit many home
runs with the Dodgers.

In 1947, Robinson was named Rookie of the Year—the biggest honor for a first-year player. He led the way for other African-American players. Soon, more players from the Negro Leagues joined major league teams. Robinson became one of the greatest baseball players the game had ever seen. His teammates and Dodgers fans came to love him.

Reese showed people Robinson
was part of the team.

Facing Discrimination

Robinson still faced discrimination, though. One day, fans for the opposing team began calling Robinson names. Dodgers team captain Pee Wee Reese walked over to Robinson. He put his arm around Robinson's shoulders. It was an act many people would remember. It showed that African Americans had every right to play baseball.

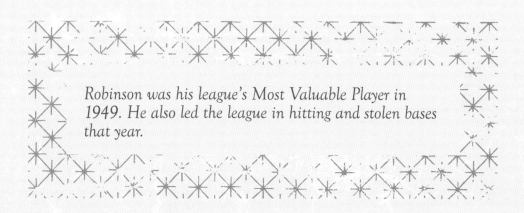

Robinson was his league's Most Valuable Player in 1949. He also led the league in hitting and stolen bases that year.

Robinson was one of the most skilled baseball players of his time. In his baseball career, Robinson played 1,382 games, hit 137 home runs, and stole 197 bases. Fans chose him to play on the National League All-Star team six times. He helped the Dodgers win six National League championships and one World Series.

Robinson retired from baseball in 1957. He was voted into the National Baseball Hall of Fame in 1962.

Rachel and Branch Rickey were with Robinson when he was voted into the National Baseball Hall of Fame.

Champion for Equality

After leaving baseball, Robinson began working more to fight for equality for African Americans. He worked with the National Association for the Advancement of Colored People (NAACP).

Robinson went all over the United States giving speeches. He talked to African Americans about self-respect. He talked about ending racism. The NAACP awarded Robinson the Spingarn Medal. Each year this award is given to an African American who is at the top in his or her field.

Robinson died on October 24, 1972. He led the life of a great champion, both on and off the baseball field.

Robinson worked to get equal rights for African Americans.

FUN FACTS

✦ From 1964 to 1968, Robinson worked on civil rights issues for the governor of New York.

✦ A postage stamp honoring Robinson was issued in 1997.

✦ As of 2010, Robinson was the only Major League Baseball player to have his uniform number retired across the league. This means that no player in Major League Baseball can wear number 42.

TIMELINE

1919 Jackie Robinson was born on January 31 in Georgia.

1935 Robinson became quarterback of his high school football team.

1939 Robinson attended UCLA, where he played varsity football, basketball, baseball, and track.

1942 Robinson joined the U.S. Army.

1945 Robinson signed with the Brooklyn Dodgers.

1946 Robinson married Rachel Isum.

1947 Robinson became the first African-American player in modern Major League Baseball.

1949 Robinson was named the National League's Most Valuable Player.

1957 Robinson retired from baseball.

1962 Robinson was voted into the National Baseball Hall of Fame.

1972 Robinson died on October 24.

1997 Major League Baseball retired Robinson's uniform number, 42.

GLOSSARY

All-Star team—a team that the best players in each league are chosen to play on in an All-Star game.

discrimination—the act of treating people unfairly because of their race, religion, or gender.

Major League Baseball—the highest league of baseball in the United States.

minor leagues—the leagues below the highest league of baseball in the United States.

National League—one of the two leagues that make up Major League Baseball; the other is the American League.

racism—the belief that one race is better than another.

retire—to stop working, usually because of age. When something is taken out of service or use, it is also retired.

scholarship—a prize that pays for some or all of a person's education.

World War II—from 1939 to 1945, fought in Europe, Asia, and Africa. Great Britain, France, the United States, the Soviet Union, and their allies were on one side. Germany, Italy, Japan, and their allies were on the other side.

LEARN MORE

At the Library

Burleigh, Robert. *Stealing Home*. New York: Simon & Schuster, 2007.

Harrison, Peggy. *We Love Baseball!* New York: Random House, 2003.

Nelson, Kadir. *We Are the Ship: The Story of Negro League Baseball*. New York: Hyperion, 2008.

On the Web

To learn more about Jackie Robinson, visit ABDO Group online at **www.abdopublishing.com**. Web sites about Robinson are featured on our Book Links page. These links are routinely monitored and updated to provide the most current information available.

INDEX